THROUGH NO FAULT OF MY OWN

Through No Fault of My Own

A Girl's Diary of Life
on Summit Avenue
in the Jazz Age

▪ Coco Irvine ▪

INTRODUCTION by
PEG MEIER

UNIVERSITY OF MINNESOTA PRESS
MINNEAPOLIS · LONDON

THE FESLER–LAMPERT MINNESOTA HERITAGE BOOK SERIES

This series reprints significant books that enhance our understanding and appreciation of Minnesota and the Upper Midwest. It is supported by the generous assistance of the John K. and Elsie Lampert Fesler Fund and the interest and contribution of Elizabeth P. Fesler and the late David R. Fesler.

Photographs are reproduced courtesy of Olivia C. Ford, unless credited otherwise.

Published by the University of Minnesota Press
111 Third Avenue South, Suite 290
Minneapolis, MN 55401-2520

http://www.upress.umn.edu

Library of Congress Cataloging-in-Publication Data

Irvine, Coco, 1914–1975.

    Through no fault of my own : a girl's diary of life on Summit Avenue in the jazz age / Coco Irvine with Peg Meier.

        p.   cm. — (The Fesler–Lampert Minnesota heritage book series)

    ISBN 978-0-8166-7306-3 (pbk. : alk. paper)

1. Irvine, Coco, 1914–1975—Diaries. 2. Teenage girls—Minnesota—St. Paul—Diaries. 3. Summit Avenue (St. Paul, Minn.)—History—20th century. 4. St. Paul (Minn.)—History—20th century. 5. St. Paul (Minn.)—Social life and customs—20th century. 6. St. Paul (Minn.)—Biography. 7. Irvine, Coco, 1914–1975—Childhood and youth. 8. Irvine, Coco, 1914–1975—Family. 9. Teenage girls—Minnesota—St. Paul—Social life and customs—20th century. I. Meier, Peg, 1946– . II. Title.

    F614.S4I78 2011
    977.6'58104—DC22

                                                              2010045811

Design and production by Mighty Media, Inc.
Text design by Chris Long

Printed in Canada on acid-free paper

The University of Minnesota is an equal-opportunity educator and employer.

18 17 16 15 14 13 12   10 9 8 7 6 5 4 3

Introduction

PEG MEIER

A MINNESOTA GIRL NAMED COCO IRVINE received a blank diary as a Christmas gift in 1926. Coco, about to turn thirteen, loved to write and loved to get into trouble, so the gift was perfect: the diary gave her a chance to explain her side of the messes she created. "I'm in deep trouble through no fault of my own" was her frequent excuse. Starting on January 1, 1927, the adventuresome Coco recorded a year's worth of her escapades, her moods, and her heartache about being ignored by a boy of her age whom she referred to as "He," usually with that capital letter.

In much of the diary, she comes off as a regular kid, if precocious. Girls today can identify with her joys and troubles as childhood melts into the tumultuous teenage years. Coco alternated between adoring and despising her parents: "I don't like my mother very much," she wrote, "but I do want her to like me." While she hated being treated as a mere child, she still loved playing with paper dolls—one of whom she imagined was pregnant and not married.

If you read attentively, you'll see hints that Coco and her family were far from ordinary. The Irvines of St. Paul, Minnesota, were among the Midwest's wealthiest families. They were Minnesota's Vanderbilts, its Rockefellers. Coco's father and his father before him owned lumber companies at the peak of the industry. She grew up in an imposing twenty-room house with nine bedrooms, eight bathrooms, and nine fireplaces. The mansion was finished in a stunning variety of elegant hardwoods, suitable for a lumberman's home. If you live in Minnesota, you may have been in Coco's house: it was donated to the state by Coco and her sister in 1965 and is now Minnesota's official Governor's Residence, sometimes open for tours.

In the 1920s, the Irvine family (pronounced ER-vin) also had a huge summer home on an island in White Bear Lake, near St. Paul, and a 360-acre horse farm near Stillwater, Minnesota. They had servants and nannies and drivers. The four Irvine children—Libby, Tom, Coco, and Olivia—were full of pranks and foolishness, but they excelled in private school and were taught proper manners. Their nursemaid,

Octavia Rocheford (whom they called "Tay"), said some forty years later, "Some [rich] children like that can be kind of snooty to their maid, but they weren't. Oh, they were wonderful children. Even the boy was so nice, Tom." The maid apparently did not dwell on the night that Tom, sixteen, and Coco, thirteen, sneaked past her and out of the house to go dancing at a ballroom, Coco wearing her mother's clothes, rouge, and high heels, the too-big shoes tied on her feet.

Coco's father, Horace, was a staunch Republican; her mother, Clotilde, was a dyed-in-the-wool Democrat. They joked that they canceled each other's vote. Conversations at Irvine family dinners often centered on politics and were heated because neither parent gave an inch. The children were expected to come to the table with something interesting to discuss, preferably about current events. Clearly, the dirty joke Coco told at the dinner table in January 1927 and recorded in her diary did not fit the bill.

The Roaring Twenties, Coco's teen years, were also known as the Jazz Age. Music, fashion, art, and literature were all in flux. Women throughout the nation finally were granted the right to vote in 1920; Minnesota women, ahead of the curve, had already been allowed to vote in some local elections. Charles

Lindbergh, who spent boyhood summers in Minnesota, electrified the world by flying across the Atlantic Ocean nonstop in May 1927 (but didn't rate a word in Coco's diary). Another rebel named Coco—Chanel, the French fashion designer—was setting the style of the 1920s "flapper girl" and challenging the concept of proper behavior.

The economy was still flying high in 1927, the year of Coco's diary. Headlines in the St. Paul newspapers in January read: "Flour production exceeds previous year," "1926 farm implement sales up 20 percent," and "Bankers hopeful as efficiency and economy increase." Houses were selling fast. Newspaper listings showed a six-room home with a sun porch on St. Paul's Capitol Avenue for sale for $6,000, only $500 down, and a duplex on Dayton's Bluff for $8,000, with "easy terms." (Mansions such as the Irvines' did not require advertisements.) Few clues forecast the stock market plunge of October 1929 and the long Depression that followed.

The Irvines' stately home at 1006 Summit Avenue, within three miles of the state capitol and the St. Paul cathedral, had the distinguished air of an old English Tudor manor house. Its gigantic carved staircase was perfect for "coming out" parties, when daughters were formally introduced to the high society that they were expected to join. Summit Avenue was the showcase of St. Paul. It was arguably the toniest street in Minnesota, lined on both sides with homes of men who had made fortunes in mining, lumber, and railroads. Mansion was built next to mansion, each with spacious grounds on the bluff looking toward the Mississippi River. When the Irvines built their $50,000 home on a nearly vacant block in 1910, four years before Coco was born, people were astonished. "Why, that's way out on the prairie," they said.

During the late 1800s and early 1900s, such celebrities as James J. Hill, founder of the Great Northern Railway, and novelist F. Scott Fitzgerald lived on Summit Avenue. People across the nation still know it as the street where the twenty-two-year-old Fitzgerald finished his first novel, *This Side of Paradise*, in 1919. When his story about young love was accepted for publication, he ran up and down Summit Avenue proclaiming the good news. Strapped for money, he lived in a third-floor room at 599 Summit Avenue and made it clear he felt crippled by not having the wealth of those residents who lived just a mile west on the same street. The Irvines lived the kind of life to which Fitzgerald aspired (as did his later character, Jay Gatsby, in *The Great Gatsby*), with dance lessons and sailboats and garden parties. In his fiction, Fitzgerald used names of real people he had known, including "Clotilde," Coco's name and that of her mother. In *This Side of Paradise*, Clothilde is a servant. We have to wonder if Fitzgerald knew of the Irvines and gave them this literary stab. He later called Summit Avenue "a mausoleum of American architectural monstrosities," which was about as negative as Frank Lloyd Wright's description of the street: "the worst collection of architecture in the world." Summit Avenue suffered during the mid-twentieth century, with houses torn down or converted to apartments, but it has recovered nicely. Some architectural historians say it is the longest remaining stretch of Victorian homes in the United States.

Coco's diary stayed in her hands, and whether her parents and siblings were aware of it in the 1920s is not known. Nor is it known if she kept diaries during other years. When she was in her midfifties and ill with a recurrence of cancer, she revisited the 1927 diary written in her girlish handwriting and prepared it for a limited publication. According to her daughter, Coco probably edited sections to omit boring pieces, which accounts for missing dates in the book. Coco couldn't type and must have hired a typist. How much she changed her diary at that time, if at all, is a mystery because the original diary cannot be found. Her daughter believes that Coco, or the typist, or the printer, threw out the original diary after it was set in type.

The diary is clearly Coco's voice. She studied writing at Sarah Lawrence College in New York, and her fiction was published in the college magazine. In 1940 her parents privately published a book of her writings as a girl and young woman, *Poems, Essays, and Other Pieces, 1925–1934*. The volume still exists and shows how Coco's writing style matured but remained similar to the diary in language and style—though lacking much of its exuberance.

In our current period of fraudulent memoirs, *Through No Fault of My Own* is believable. It's a child's diary, not a memoir written later in life, and it gives us a teenage girl's charming view of the world. It reveals what it's like to be smitten with love and how it feels to be snubbed. The diary, even if edited by the author many years later, conveys a time and place and attitude. Like Anne Frank's Holocaust-era diary, which Anne reworked before her death, Coco's journal presents the words of a teenage girl with natural writing talent.

Coco's diary may not have experienced this renaissance if not for her younger sister, Olivia Irvine Dodge. When Coco was ill in the summer of 1975, Olivia picked up the diary project; she had a hardcover version privately printed, making about one hundred copies for family and friends as Christmas gifts. Coco died that summer, before the book was off the press. One copy made its way to the Minnesota Historical Society archives, where I happened on it. I remember sitting in the somber library, trying not to guffaw as I read about Coco's exploits. This edition published by the University of Minnesota Press is unchanged except for corrections of a few typographical errors.

I hope you enjoy Coco's stories and adventures as much as I do. And when you have read the diary, I'll tell you who Coco married and what became of her. No peeking or jumping ahead!

THROUGH NO FAULT OF MY OWN

Dear Diary,

This is to be my most private account of everything that happens to me.

NO ONE MUST READ A WORD FURTHER
UNDER PAIN OF DEATH.
A CURSE SHALL BEFALL ANY
WHO DISREGARD THIS WARNING.

Everything is getting quite different in my life because of boys! I absolutely like one now. I guess he likes me, too. This diary is to keep track of how things go, so I can analyze the best way of making certain he likes me. He sure acts like he doesn't, which is a good sign.

Clotilde Emily Irvine
"CoCo"

Saturday, January 1, 1927

I got this diary for Christmas. I will write here a few things I remember from my youth. I was born January 27, 1914, at 11:30 at night. This is hearsay as I do not remember, being too young at the time. At this period of my life I had a sister five years old and a brother nearly four years old. Later I got another sister. I was a fat, unattractive baby (judging from pictures) of a very stubborn disposition. When I was three I threw up all over Mother because she made me eat apricots. She still remembers this. So do I.

I remember when my little sister was born. Up until that time I had gone by the name of "Baby." I truly thought that was my real name. A horrible girl named Dot lives next door and is older even than my sister Lib. She asked me what my name was. I answered, Baby Irvine. She shouted triumphantly, "Oh no IT ISN'T. There is a new baby at your house now." My sister said, "Shut up, Dot. Her name is Clotilde like our mother." This was news to me. I knew I could never remember such a name and I was humiliated. I have never forgotten this gruesome experience.

As soon as this new baby could walk my mother made me dress like her. This horrible experience continued until last fall when *thankfully* I entered seventh grade and had to wear a uniform. It seems a cruel shame to make a person suffer so. I still have humiliating problems like having to wear long underwear all winter. Nearly nobody else has to. My little sister's name is Olivia. She never was known as Baby after all except when being teased.

This is about all you need to know about my past, Diary, except one more thing. When I was nine, the person I loved most died. She was my grandmother. I felt very tragic about it and still do. I like my family most of the time. Not always. This boy I like goes to Sunday school. I have known him many years but never knew I really liked him til I started dancing school last fall. Friday is dancing school night.

Friday, January 7

Dancing school night. Hope He will be there!

Later: He was. He danced with everyone but me. That's a good sign because even tho he didn't dance with me He looked at me three times. I had fun with Charlie. He told me this joke, which I find humorous. *A dog went across the railroad track and a train ran over his tail. He looked back to see where his tail was and a train came the other way and cut off his head. Moral: Don't lose your head over a little piece of tail.*

I danced three times with Charles, six times with Bobby, and four times with George, and that's all. Only I don't like them too much—they are valuable only as people who can keep me from being stuck. I have to cultivate as many people as possible so that won't ever happen.

Sunday, January 9

I am in deep trouble through no fault of my own. I told the funny joke at the dinner table and Daddy took great exception to it. I said as plaintively as possible, "What's wrong with it?"

Daddy in a *most emphatic* way said, "It is not a good joke for a child your age and please don't repeat it."

"But what does it mean?" I asked, ignoring his reference to my childhood, which if he had any brains he would see is a thing of the past.

He said feebly, looking at Mother, "Well, it just means going on a little party." There is something more to this than just that, for what's wrong with that? I mean to find out.

Last night I went skating at the University Club rink. *He* was there! I was wearing my red jacket and cap. I was practicing my figure eights, which I don't know how to do very well, when He came skating up to me. He said, "You look like Red Riding Hood and you know what happened to her. The wolf came and ate her all up"—and he made a horrible face at me. "He'd have to catch her first!" I said, skating away nearly as fast as I could. He came after me and of course caught me, being good at hockey. He grabbed me around the waist and I thought he was going to kiss me and I tried to decide whether to let him. He didn't, though. He pushed me away and skated as fast as anything around and round the rink. Showing off, I guess. This was all very romantic.

Today was Lib's birthday. I made her a nightgown out of an old sheet at sewing class and put her initials on in pink thread. I guess she didn't like it. I heard her describing it in a derogatory manner on the telephone to a friend of hers. The *nerve*. I worked hard on it. I didn't eat any of her cake. I don't think she noticed. Well, she leaves to go back to boarding school tomorrow. She was nice about it when I took the quarter out of her purse and Mother caught me. She even told Mother she had said I could. (She hadn't.) I don't forget kindnesses done me. They are few and far between.

Wednesday, January 12

In the worst trouble I've ever been in, still through no fault of my own. I can *not* understand it. Daddy and Mother were going to a dinner party. They were all dressed up so I yelled over the banister, "Where are you going? Is it a little piece of tail?" Daddy grew thunderously angry and came up the stairs two at a time and actually *shook* me. I was grievously hurt and went in my room and locked the door. What can it all mean? Wait til I see that Charlie. Of all the *nerve*!

Friday, January 14

Dancing school night. The second Charlie danced with me I accused him of getting me in all this trouble at home. He was mystified when I told him all about it. I said it must be a terribly awful joke. He said it was, but it is obvious to me that he hasn't the faintest idea why any more than I do. It is good tho, because now we have a secret together and across the room we wag our finger at each other like a tail. And then of course we have it to talk about so he kept coming back and back, cutting in on me and I got very popular as anyone could see they weren't going to get stuck with me. Maybe it was the best thing that could have happened in spite of everything!

He didn't dance with me til the very end. He said, "You seem to be awfully clubby with Charlie." I said, "Well, you never dance with me, so I have to amuse myself somehow." He said, "Oh, but I save you for the last." I said, "Is that a compliment?" He said, "You should know" but I still don't. A person could take that as either yes or no. It is most *aggravating*.

Grandpa's birthday. We had cake.

Saturday, January 15

We all went skating tonight and then back to my house. We played Truth and Consequences and Winkum, both of which entail kissing. It can be fun if you know how to do it right. In Winkum you have to look at a boy in a certain way and then wink at someone else. This is aggravating to the first boy, who thinks you plan to let him kiss you, and a joyous surprise to the person you wink at. I tried this on three boys and fear I made three friends and three enemies. Maybe it isn't such a good idea. I winked at Charlie twice (I owe it to him for the joke and dancing with me and all) and once at *him*. *He* didn't seem at all surprised. In Truth and Consequences I asked him who he liked best of girls. He said he hated them all and what did I think of that? It was 11:30 P.M. before I got to bed. I was so tired.

Sunday, January 16

A queer thing happened this morning. Tom and I were in his bed reading the funnies. We have done this since I was young and nobody ever said a thing. This morning for reasons unknown to me, Mother came into Tom's room (usually she is still asleep at this time) and became exercised over the fact that we were reading the funnies. She said, "Tom Irvine, you know better than this." I said, "Why Mother, we always do this. What's wrong with the funnies?" She said, "It isn't that and Tom should know if you don't." Tom said, "For heaven's sake, Mother!" He was very mad. Mother said, "It was different when you were children but now that Clotilde"—she always calls me Clotilde, never Coco—"is growing up I don't want this to happen again." I asked, "What? Can't we read the funnies?" Mother said, "You know perfectly well what I mean" and stalked away. I said to Tom, "What's ailing her? Is she crazy?" Tom didn't answer at all. He was white with rage. Naturally I know I'm growing up, in fact I'm a lot smarter than some people think. In fact, I'm smarter than most people in this family. If people would say what they are talking about maybe even I could understand.

Then a sinister thing occurred. Mother called me into her room and wanted to talk about the facts of life, of all things. She asked me if I knew where babies come from. I told her disdainfully that I did. (I have for ever so long, through no fault of hers.) She asked me if I understood why it wasn't quite nice for me to be in Tom's bed. I said I didn't and she explained quite kindly that since he was a boy and I was a girl it just wasn't right. Ye Gods, I wouldn't read funnies in bed with just any boy. I can see that and wouldn't dream of such a thing. But my brother! Honestly!

Tuesday

School! The less said about that the better. My marks are awful and if I get a card (meaning *work not satisfactory*) Mother threatens I can't go to dancing school next week. I figure I'm bound to get a card but figure also that she will never keep me home from dancing school as said occasion falls near my birthday. Even she could not be so cruel.

Wednesday

Daddy returned from away. This evening I heard
Mother talking about me to him in a derogatory way.
He said, "Good Lord, Clover, she's nothing but a child,
why put ideas in her head!" If only he knew, I have
plenty of ideas in my head. I know plenty of interesting things and if necessary I will run away and find
out anything I don't already know about. So there!

January 28

Yesterday was my thirteenth birthday. I got a card,
of course, but this is Friday after my birthday and
dancing school night so just as I suspected Mother,
not being a fiend, let me go. She gave me a new dancing school dress which is actually sleeveless. A great
concession! Also it is not pink or blue (like usual)
but green taffeta. I look really old in it except for my
feet. She made me wear my same black patent leath-
ers. She says high heels are absolutely out because I
would break my neck. Tom gave me a compact. Lib
sent a telegram and Daddy gave me $10.00. A *very*
satisfactory day. At dancing school all the girls were
pea-green with envy and made derogatory remarks
about sleeveless dresses. I was amused to see Dotty

and Dede wore their dotted swisses! (Really childish.) Dede's even had a sash. Imagine! I had the best time. Everyone danced with me, even *him*, though he had to ruin it all by remarking, "Even I don't feel I can ignore you on your birthday." I don't know how I can stand him and told him so. He said, "Who's asking you to?" Ye Gods!

Monday

My sister Olivia is very smart in some ways for a person only eight years old. I can always tell when she is going to get out of going to school the next day. I will find her engrossed in some book of *Les Malheurs de Sophie*, which she is learning to read in French. Sure enough the next morning she is making strange sounds in her throat and wrapped up in cloths of Vix, reading comfortably in bed while I have to trudge to school through a driving blizzard. This fills me with wrath for I always know when I return home she will be fully recovered and perfectly capable of pestering the daylights out of me until after supper, when she of course has a severe relapse (like fun). This is the smart part of her. The dumb part is that Tom and I can get away with murder by bribing her not to tell on us. The strange thing is that all we need to give her

is a few sheets of smooth tissue paper and she will
remain silent as the grave. If only she knew there are
quantities of this paper in the attic, or were. (Tom and
I have now hidden it and dole it out a little at a time
when necessary.)

The last time this was necessary was last fall.
Mother and Daddy had gone to New York and Tom
and I were really full of vim. We were all left in the
jurisdiction of Grandpa (who lives here but is deaf)
and Tay, who is Olivia's nurse. (She has nothing to
do with me. I don't even walk to school with her and
Olivia, but take the long way so no one will get the
idea I have anything to do with that mere child and
her nurse.) Anyway, Tom thought it would be a good
time for us to go to the Oxford Ballroom and dance one
night. I agreed but wondered how we could. He said,
"Just pretend you are sick. Go to bed early. Grandpa
won't know the difference and Tay won't check on you
once she thinks you are asleep." I agreed to all but
wondered what I was to wear as my clothes are all so
childish still. He took me to Mother's dressing room
and we picked out one outfit, which tho much too big
(I have grown some since then) at least stayed on. The
shoes were the hard part but we figured we could tie
them on some way. Tom snitched some rouge and lip-

stick out of her (Mother's) drawer and we were going to hide all this stuff in the downstairs john so I could sneak down and get dressed and then we could escape out of the side door. The Oxford Ballroom is only a block away on Grand Avenue so that was no problem.

All was settled and we turned to find this fiendish face of my sister Olivia staring out of long curls saying, "What'll you give me if I don't tell?" My heart was in my feet at this unlooked-for hindrance but Tom offered her six sheets of smooth shiny paper for her silence. He put it in such a way that the paper looked attractive even to me! My sister complied to all requirements and everything went just as peachy as could be. Tay, who has nothing to do with me except see that I get in bed at the proper time, believed me when I went to bed with a headache at eight o'clock. I got up at a quarter of nine, went downstairs past Grandpa's room (who, you know, is deaf), and Tom helped me to dress in Mother's clothes in the downstairs bathroom. He was discouraged with my appearance even with the rouge and all. He thought I looked still too young. And the shoes were awful to keep on. Anyway, we went and had a marvelous time. I have danced with Tom since I was ten and we can do almost any step together. At one time all the people stood and clapped for us. (I had to take Mother's shoes off and then everything was just perfect.) Some people laughed but we paid little or no attention to such rudeness. We went home, got in safely, and thought that was the end of that.

It wasn't, tho. It seems that the tailor on the corner had seen Tom and me that night and unbeknownst to us was a person who passed the time of day with Grandpa. He told him (Grandpa), who isn't that deaf, that he better watch those Irvine kids. He didn't like to see little girls out late at night dressed for Halloween even if with their brother. Grandpa thundered home. He was waiting for us on our return from school. He ordered us to our rooms (forgetting there is a connecting passageway between them) and told us we must stay there for the weekend. This was hard on Tom but not on me as I don't have dates yet. He has millions.

I was not worried Grandpa would tell Mother and Daddy. After all, he should have caught us *before* this happened. I pointed this out to Tom and he felt better. I had a nice weekend. We played "Blue Room" and "Molly and Me" and all those good pieces on the Victrola. Tom was sad because he didn't even dare violate Grandpa's ultimatum and sneak out again. Tay was nice and gave us lemonade whenever we wanted and never reminded Grandpa about the passage between our rooms. I like to believe Grandpa knew of this but, not being a cruel man, pretended he didn't.

February 1

Awful old school. At lunch we had codfish balls and old dead salad. I told Jeanie we could not go on this way and we must do something about our lunches or we would starve. She asked "What?" and I answered darkly, "I'll think of something."

February 3

I thought of something—but it ended in our getting suspended from all classes today and not even being allowed to have recess or lunch hour. We were put in separate rooms for the whole day, and they plan to have a meeting to discuss what to do with us. All this over practically nothing.

All we did was wait til school was out yesterday. We hid in the cloakroom til everyone had left (we thought) and then we took all the knives and forks and spoons we could carry. (We put them in our pockets and in our bloomers and any place that would hold them.) We were planning to hide them, not steal them and sell them or anything like that—only to hide them so we would have to go home for lunch until they could afford to buy new ones. It seemed like an innocent enough solution to the problem of how not to have to eat that awful food.

Disasterously, as we were coming up the stone stairs, the rubber in Jeanie's bloomers broke and knives, forks, and spoons went clattering down the stairs. I couldn't help but laugh, but only briefly, for who should appear at the head of the stairs but Miss Holler. Words fail me. My despair was utterly complete. She, of course, saw no humor in the situation, having no sense of humor herself. She told us that she knew we were uncooperative but it never occurred to her we were thieves (imagine) and that this was the worst deed which had ever transpired at Summit School and that our parents would be informed. Then she told us to go home after putting back every single knife, fork, and spoon in its proper place. She stood grimly over us while this took place. Today she gave us strict instructions to be in our seats at 8:30 tomorrow when Miss Converse (our principal) would deal with our punishment. She (Miss Holler) claimed she would not be surprised if we were expelled!

Thankfully Mother and Daddy are in the East.

February 4

They had the meeting about us yesterday after school, and this morning Miss Converse told us we would not be expelled but would be suspended for one week. I argued that my marks were bad enough without missing a week of classes and she said, "You should have thought of that." Then for the rest of the term til Easter we cannot have recess or lunch period with the rest of the school, but must eat alone—not even with each other. After school almost everyone in the class called me up. The majority feel a grave injustice has been done us. Some said they would have done the same thing had they thought of it. Jeanie and I feel it would have all been worthwhile if the lunches had improved. They didn't, though, so we are martyred for nothing. Mother and Daddy get home tomorrow—
HELP!

February 5

They got back this morning. I decided I better tell them all before anyone else did, so I met them at the door, crying. It was not all put on either, as I was really scared nearly out of my mind. Daddy can be quite fierce and Mother gets mad at much less than this.

Well, I worked myself into a good case of hysterics and cried so hard I couldn't talk. They got scared and probably thought I had found I had an incurable disease or something. Daddy kept saying, "Come on now, nothing can be as bad as all that." Finally I decided they would probably forgive me anything they were so scared I would die of hysterics.

They were very kind about it and decided I was being punished enough at school and I can even go to dancing school on Friday. It pays to know how to manage things. If I had been defiant, things might have had a disastrous turn for the worse. As it is I feel so peaceful I can even enjoy being a martyr now. Daddy said he didn't approve of children being kept from their classmates for so long a period. He may talk to Miss Converse about it. I ate a huge breakfast, nearly my first food since all this began. I don't even object to Daddy thinking me a child. Sometimes I wish I were one. Life is simpler for them.

Monday

His mother called my mother and said there was to be a party at Billy Bussel's on Saturday and that if Mother agreed, she (his mother) would pick me up at 7:30 and bring me home at 10:00. I am so excited. This is nearly like a date.

Wednesday

Can't study or anything. I'm so excited over Saturday.

Friday

Went to movies—*My Best Girl*. Buddy Rogers (so cute) and Mary Pickford. Ish. I bet she's 25 and still wears curls like Olivia.

Saturday

The most devastating thing happened. Jeanie was teaching me to stand on my head (it was a way of passing the time until tonight). I was getting good at it but lost my balance and my feet came down on a straight chair. I shrieked with pain and Jeanie ran to get Mother. Mother called the doctor and my toe is broken. I can't go to the party. Thankfully they think it is the pain that makes me cry. It partly is.

Tom came home and laughed at me til I cried some more. I am the first person he ever heard of who broke her toe while standing on her head. Later he gave me five new movie magazines he hadn't even read yet.

Sunday

First thing this morning I called Dotty and asked her about the party. She said it was super. She said she danced with him four times, she said they danced and played games and had refreshments. All this while I lay here in dire pain. She said she wore a new dress and that she knew Mickey liked her. She said she was very popular (who cares?) and she said everyone knew why I wasn't there and laughed and laughed. My humiliation is complete. I am the most unfortunate of women.

Sunday

A very sinister thing has turned up in my family. It appears my mother is gambling on the stock market. She has been taking her winnings from Mah Jongg and also some of her own personal funds and buying something by the name of Kennecott Copper. I heard Daddy thundering at Mother in the library. Daddy said in no uncertain terms "all women are damn fools and you're no exception."

Mother was naturally righteously indignant at being sworn at by one who should hold her dear. For once I was on Mother's side. I wonder if I couldn't do something like this if only I could save some money. I get only $5.00 a month. Daddy lets me spend it as I wish. He puts five $1.00 bills in the drawer of the desk. I may take $1.00 a week or all at once but when it is gone, that's all for the rest of the time. It is a devastating thing to find you are bankrupt before the first week is over. This happens almost always as it seems like so much money at first, but it isn't. If I have any money left over at the end of the month, Daddy says he will double what is left plus my allowance. This hasn't happened yet. I have lots of expenses. Tom always has to borrow (tho he does pay back).

It is a weird thing but I am again in grave trouble through practically no fault of my own, as usual. It seems I was merely bouncing a basketball against the wall. It wasn't my fault that it inadvertently hit the fire alarm and caused all the rumpus. Honestly, it could have happened to anyone. But as Miss Converse (our principal) pointed out, just anyone would not have been bouncing the ball exactly in that spot. I had to agree with her on that, as most everyone I know is the worst kind of sissy and they don't have the least idea of how exciting it is to hope very much with one side of you that the ball will hit the fire alarm and the other side is scared to death it will!

I have to admit that although I didn't plan this, it came at a fortunate time. My next class was French. I was totally unprepared, and so I reasoned if the ball did just happen to hit the fire alarm it would be fate saving me from a fate worse than death. I am not sorry it happened, though I was really dismayed when I saw people from all parts of the school filing out in perfect order as we have been rehearsed so often. I did wonder what horrible recompense was in store for me.

Sure enough, I found out very soon. We were all congregated in front of the school, and Miss Converse said, "Silence." The whole school was still, and Miss Converse said severely, "Who did this childish prank?" I knew perfectly I would be the first suspect, so I said meekly, "I did, Miss Converse." She ascertained my assumption by saying, "I thought so." I blessed my boots I had been forthright and honest about the whole thing. She then said, "You will go to my office and remain there til I come. Rest of the school, go to your classes." I slunk away to her office, half happy I wasn't in French but mostly not. After what seemed a few years, the faculty came in her office. No one spoke a word but looked disdainfully at poor me. I thought of running out quickly and leaving home and school for good, but it was snowing outside and I have only 13 cents left of my last allowance. I supposed that this would be the last straw and that surely I was to be expelled for sure, but such was not the case.

Miss Converse eventually appeared. She looked compassionately at me and asked me to follow her out of the office, which I did. She said, "I did not intend to subject you to a faculty meeting. What you did was childish in the extreme and not worthy of such atten- tion. In the future if you want to ring the fire alarm you may, but first ask me so I can plan a fire drill at that time." I was so deflated I almost cried. Then she said, "Enough of this foolishness. Now go to your class." I didn't even miss much French, and I didn't even have a chance to tell her that maybe it wasn't exactly on purpose.

I was really sick for two days. It started as if I weren't at all. Olivia, as usual, had her croup. She pretends only half the time. Somehow they actually believed me when I said I had chills and I was allowed to stay home from school. They put Olivia and me in Mother and Daddy's room with Olivia's nurse to look after us. It was a snowy, cold morning and I was looking forward to reading my good book. I didn't even feel like it. Most surprising! Then I thought if Tay read to Olivia that would be nice. I didn't even like that! Tay took my temperature all the time. Finally she left the room and Mother, who had gone out for lunch, came home at once. I was so sick I hurt all over. She was making clucking noises like she does when nervous. I said, "Mother, don't give me carbolic acid." Mother said, "Lie still, dear." The doctor came and made me have a cold enema to take down my temperature, much against my will. I had a trained nurse all night. Mother woke me up three times to see I was all right. Daddy said this morning, "Well, you did give us a scare, Miss Trouble."

Honestly! As Mother says, sometimes men don't know anything.

There is much I find wrong with my life. Like I am not given any credit for being an exceptionally intelligent person for my age—or even Mother's, for that matter. I know, for instance, what I am perfectly capable of doing that she has no idea of. Such as, for instance, I can manage everything, even her, in a way in which she has no idea of. I know how she gets Daddy mad and I can see just how she could get away with things if only she didn't have to argue all the time. Daddy can't stand people to cry—that means, therefore, if she would cry instead of fighting she would ergo (therefore) get her own way. I do. Like tonight. (I figure I can always be a great actress unless I decide to be something else. I can cry whenever necessary, out-talk anyone unless I find it expedient not to, and be completely obnoxious if I feel like it. I may, of course, prefer to be a great writer. I know all the words I need to, however I need more experience, which I see no immediate way of getting at this moment since I don't know any boys who have as much brains or experience vicariously as I do.)

It came back to me how, long ago, when I was only six, my mother actually tried to murder me. She gave me carbolic acid, which was undiluted, for my ear and made me eat it as a laxative. I could have died but didn't and only threw up all over the taxi instead. Daddy was indignant. It seems we were on our way home from Hyannisport. We had taken a ferry boat across the sound or whatever it was. Anyway we stayed in Boston overnight and Mother stayed home with me next day, while Daddy took the rest of us to the zoo or something. Mother longed to cure me rapidly of the earache and suddenly gave me this poison. She realized her mistake almost at once and, telling me apprehensively to stay where I was, she rushed to the desk, pushing the people aside, announcing she had poisoned her daughter. People raced from everywhere and a doctor was procured. He stuck his finger down my throat and gave me Epicak. This unfortunately worked on me for many hours. I was so sick! It was so cruel of a person to do such to her helpless child. Daddy was really mad, mainly because I ruined the taxi and he had to pay extra.

I happen to remember an amusing incident which took place last summer. I did not participate in this occurrence, having been shipped off to Madeline Island in Wisconsin, ostensibly because of hay fever but probably mainly to get rid of me. Believe me, they won't get me back there this year. They sent me with Dotty and a lady named Mrs. Hollingshead. I was so homesick and it did nothing but rain all the whole time. However, this is neither here nor there about what happened while I was gone. It seems Tom had bought some kind of gadget that fits on a radio and will cut off the music or whatever is going on. Then he (Tom) could cut in on the program and announce any news he wanted. My sister Lib, who is of an excitable disposition, was home. Also my sister Olivia, who carried things too far being too young to know better. We have two radios, one upstairs and one downstairs.

Mother and Daddy were in the library when Olivia came hurtling down the stairs screaming, "Mother, Daddy, turn on the radio! The President has been assassinated!" Daddy leapt to the radio, white with dismay, but he could not get the program, of course, because Tom was upstairs doing this trick. My sister Lib raced upstairs and soon came down lamenting, "It's true, it's true. I just heard the report myself." Daddy said, "Damn," turned off his radio, and Mother and he raced upstairs, followed by Lib. Olivia was screaming up and down the stairs. Tom broke in on a musical program from where he was hidden in the bathroom and announced further details on the dastardly act. Daddy moaned, "This is the worst thing since Lincoln was assassinated." Mother wept, "Mr. Coolidge was a good man, though silent." Then they left the room.

Daddy actually called the head of the bank, asking what he knew of the calamity. Mr. Prince, the president of the bank, had of course heard nothing but said he would contact the papers. The papers knew nothing but said they would contact Washington. Mother called all her friends. Olivia never told Tom things had gone so far and finally she began to get nervous. She told Tom, who turned white with fear. "Go at once," he said, "and tell them it is a joke!" Olivia did, and Daddy claimed their irresponsible idea of humor was a very serious thing and who knew what repercussions there might be. Olivia was made to call Mr. Prince of the bank and apologize. Mr. Prince, who was in the humiliating situation of having made a fool of himself, was not too pleased. Mother then tried to call the people she had told about this but their telephone lines were busy. This is all to show that I am not the only instigator of trouble at our house. I wasn't even there and look what happened. If I had been there, I would never have let things go so far.

Some of the boys my age did a terrible thing and the most awful part about it is that my brother Tom may inadvertently have been caught involved in a clandestine act. It all happened last Thursday night. (I found out about it at dancing school on Friday night.) Well, you see, it's Easter Vacation and so the older kids have been having dates all week. They all have this hangout on the Mississippi River Boulevard where they drink spiked beer. That's bad enough, but they also neck in cars. My brother is now taking out a very surreptitious girl who might not even mind. Anyway these young kids my age found out about what was going on and rode their bikes out there while supposedly at a movie. They spied on them and are writing a report on what they saw, such as who was with who and how they were getting along. The young ones are actually going to blackmail the people they saw. I am so worried. If Tom were among them (and I think he was) he's going to be blackmailed and since my friends are doing it, it will reflect back on me. He will kill me and it's not my fault! Damn!

Anyway I tried to find out how deep his involvement is but he would tell me nothing, only saying he was minding his own business Thursday night, which was none of mine. I beseeched him to tell me all as he might be involved in dire trouble, but he only said, "What do you think I was doing?" I wouldn't dare guess, but I think I know and I think he knows I know. I'm going to be the one who's really in trouble knowing these wretched people who are perpetuating the crime of blackmail. Woe is me.

I didn't have fun at dancing school because I was so worried. I don't neck and I don't think I would even if I had the chance, but since Tom stopped seeing Arline (because he saw her kiss another boy—kissing is not as serious a demeanor as necking) he has been seeing this other girl who, it is common knowledge, does neck. She even says so, and does both horizontally and vertically (whatever that means). My brother

Tom is not one to pass up opportunities, that I know. More about this later, no doubt.

May

A queer thing happened today. Miss Converse (our principal) called Mother and asked if she would bring me to school Saturday to take tests to see if I needed *tutoring*. My mother agreed. Help!

Saturday

What a day! I took these queer tests which were only questions like what do you like to do instead of finishing homework. Good Lord! I couldn't answer that with Mother probably going to read what I said. I put down I liked to read Poe and K. Mansfield depending on the time of day. Naturally there are other things I like to do, like be with friends and discuss various matters and all that. Another question was how do you outline a book. My answer was that I thought that was a dumb way to read a book. (I knew they meant Ancient History.) I said you (meaning me) lose all interest if you have to spend all that time making an outline of it when if you could read it right through it certainly is interesting.

Then there was a vocabulary test, and you crossed off words til you got the right definition (that was easy) and a few puzzles, which I think I mostly got. What a dumb test.

Mother took me home and told me Miss Converse felt I was perfectly capable of doing good work at school but I was not applying myself. She asked me if I had answered the questions honestly. I told Mother I was a very honest woman, and Mother stated I was hopeless. I said, "Mother, I would not be facetious on a test." Mother stared into space. I don't like my mother very much but I do want her to like me. I very much want her to but I will not give in. She only likes Lib, who is pretty, and Olivia, who is pretty, and Tom, who is the only boy. (She doesn't like him too much either, but she's getting him a boat for this summer. Tom will give me the rowboat.)

June 6

School's out and tomorrow we move to the lake. Oh boy! Tom is going to fix up the rowboat with a sail and sideboards for me. I can't wait. It means I will have transportation whenever I want to go over to the Club, which is directly across White Bear Lake from us. This will positively make my summer because all the Dellwood kids hang around the Yacht Club and He lives in Dellwood and has a "C" boat but this rowboat is better than nothing. I have named it "Turtle" as I suppose it won't go too fast. Also if it tips over it will turn Turtle and not go only on its side like real sailboats do.

Tonight I went to the Oxford Movie House with Tom. We saw *Seventh Heaven*, Charles Farrell and Janet Gaynor. So sad I cried and cried. He goes blind and she takes care of him. There is a marvelous tune called "Diane" running all through it.

June 9

My boat is ready! I have to use an oar for a rudder, as the rudder Tom fixed for me didn't have the capacity to turn the boat. Tayloe and I sailed all day and didn't get home in time for dinner as the wind went down and we were becalmed. It wasn't my fault but Mother was mad and said if I went gallivanting all over the lake I must take the responsibility of getting home in time for meals. Also I must always ask permission as she does not want me to use my judgment as to whether it is too windy. Honestly and really such an exasperation. How would she know better than I?

June 30

Yesterday Tom let me be his crew in the race. So far he has done very well, having two firsts in the Wednesday series and a first and second in the Sunday series. It all ended in disaster.

There was this big wind and we should have had another person. Everyone else had two crew but he thinks he's so smart. I am a very capable crew. In fact, not bragging or anything, I am the best there is though too light for such a wind (I don't weigh 100 pounds yet). Anyway, I was riding the sideboards, trying to hold the boat down. We were an easy first and I was proved. However, pride should not be felt until victory is an accomplished fact. So my feet slipped (this was not my fault as I was soaking wet and my feet were cold)—it could have happened to anyone. I fell into the lake and cried out in dismay, "Sail on, sail on, I will swim to shore." Tom was coming about to pick me up. "Go on, Tom," I shrieked, noticing about five boats passing him at once. He was swearing, I could tell, but fortunately the wind carried his words away until he got close to me. Then I heard him say in tones of wrath, "You God damn little fool, do you think I'd pick you up if I didn't have to come in with my full crew or forfeit the race?" I was mad then, too, for I figured I had made a noble gesture in practically offering to drown so he could win that stupid race. He hauled me aboard and called me a son of a bitch. I said, *"If I'm one so are you. We have the same mother."* (I had been waiting for weeks for a chance to make this remark, which I had read in a book.) We finished the race in silence, coming in next to last. This happened yesterday and we haven't spoken to each other since. Well, Mr. Smarty, it will be a long time before I will ever crew for you again, so there! In fact, I never will! Honestly!

July 2

A very exasperating thing happened today. I was eating an apple when the doorbell rang. I was only expecting Dotty so I continued eating the apple as I opened the door. Here stood this attractive man. I thought he must be some kind of salesman so I just stood staring at him and eating the apple still. He blinked his eyes at me in a fascinating sort of way. I put my hand behind me, trying to hide the apple and wipe my mouth at the same time. I noticed my dress was not my most childish, but nearly. "You must be Clotilde," he said. "Is your sister here?" I gulped and tripped on the stairs in my haste to get Lib. His name is Creighton Churchill. A most romantic name. Later Lib told me that he said he found me charming. No one has ever thought me charming before. If only I hadn't been eating that apple. I wonder if he wouldn't have thought me fascinating then, as well as charming. Damn!

Lib has many beaux. She is a very sophisticated girl with a figure like a grand slam bid and made. (This is how one of Daddy's bridge-playing friends described her.) She has blue eyes the color of forget-me-nots and smooth black hair. (My hair is only brown.) She has lots of "it," which is sex appeal plus mysterious other ingredients.

Well, all of these beaux of hers like to play tricks on each other, to make the one she seems to like look in a detrimental way. One night last week Lib went out with a boy named Alec Seymour. He is really a man, almost. He brought Lib home an hour later than he was meant to. Mother was fortunately asleep so knew nothing of this. The following morning Mother was called to the phone, where a voice was heard to say, "This is Alec Seymour. I would like to come up and see you as soon as possible." Mother made a clucking noise in her throat which shows she's nervous and told him she could see him at once. Unbeknownst to Mother this voice was not Alec at all, but a beau of Lib's by name of Peewee Milton, who is a sort of ventriloquist. Soon Alec arrived at the door. It seems Peewee had called him too and pretended he was Mother and told him she wanted to see him "at once." Alec never doubted it was Mother, as he felt guilty about bringing Lib in so late. Shaking, he came to the door, where Mother met him and politely asked him to come in and sit down. He did and there they sat, each waiting for the other to say what it was all about. After twenty minutes of this, Alec rose and left, forgetting his hat. Later I heard Mother tell Daddy that Alec Seymour was the strangest young man she had ever known and told him of her queer time with him. Daddy snorted and allowed he didn't know what the world was coming to. These young punks had lots to learn. I think that was a really good joke. I wish I'd thought of it.

Daddy says if you are afraid of something you should face up to it. I don't know where he got this weird idea because I don't believe in it at all. If it were true, rabbits and creatures like that would be fighting with wolves and things instead of running away, which is the only sensible thing for them to do. Otherwise they would be eaten all the quicker.

Today Creighton Churchill came to pick up Lib again. I saw him through the window and I was absolutely panic-stricken. I longed to open the door for him but didn't dare as I couldn't think of a single charming thing to say. I ran upstairs and hid until they were safely gone. Then I was sorry, but I still think my instinct was right. It would be disastrous if the only person in the world who thinks me charming should find out I'm actually not. Maybe by the next time he comes I will have thought of something very clever and worldly to say. I have been reading a magazine of Tom's called *Captain Billy's Whiz Bang*. Maybe I can find some anecdote in it I can relate to him.

Creighton Churchill came to pick up Lib again tonight. I knew he was coming and vowed I would not again be cowardly but come down and greet him in a normal sort of way. I had learned several anecdotes and some jokes from *Whiz Bang*, all by heart, which are rather risqué and believed he would find them amusing. I put on my green dancing school dress because I look nice in it and went downstairs so I could answer the door when he came. Unfortunately Mother and Daddy were in the living room, which is just beside the front door. Mother immediately demanded to know what I was doing in my best dress. I told her

I had decided to dress for dinner. I knew this would baffle her as usually I won't even wash my face unless made to. I was right, she just looked at me speculatively and said no more. The doorbell rang and I dignifiedly said I would answer it. There was Creighton Churchill. He said, "Hello, you dear thing" and gave me a hug. "I see you finished your apple." But he said it in such a kindly way I didn't feel absurd at all. I just felt that I didn't need to tell him all those stories from *Whiz Bang* (which was fortunate as I can't imagine what trouble I would have had with Daddy had I done such). I felt so at home with him that I talked in my normal way and I even forgot to call down Lib (I didn't want to anyway). Finally Daddy suggested I do so. I did. As they were leaving he hugged me again and kissed the top of my head. "Now don't grow up too fast. I'm going to California tomorrow but when I get back I want to see you still eating apples as if they are the most important thing in the world." It is queer the lonely feeling I had when he left.

Lib says she likes him, but finds she is in awe of him as he is very intellectual. But I don't see how this can be as he finds me charming and I don't even have a figure like a grand slam bid and made. I don't even have one like two clubs not made and yet he thinks me charming. Maybe I am intellectual but I don't think so, judging from my marks at school. Anyway, all I've got is this charm I never knew about. I wish he weren't going away. I feel just like Sentry, our dog, must feel when we all go on a trip and he knows we are going and there is nothing in the world he can do to stop us. Poor Sentry.

July 3

Went to the Yacht Club dance. We "youngsters" are made to dance upstairs as we are too noisy for the older people. Everyone goes to this dance from 12 year olds up to older than Mother and Daddy. I like to dance upstairs as no one can spy on us and get mad when we race around instead of just dancing. I hardly ever race, though. I often wish to, but feel it too undignified.

Anyway there is a boy who is known as Bellhop Jack. He is older than we and has to wear a uniform and sit behind the desk at the Club and have no fun at all, but only watch us. He must be maybe fifteen and is ugly with pimply skin and limp hair. I felt sorry for him and asked him if he would like to dance a little. He asked if I thought it would be all right and I assured him it would. I was glad when the dance was

over. He is not nice to talk to and can't dance at all.
However, it was a good deed to do. I had fun the rest
of the time. *He* danced with me many times but each
time pretended he had gotten me by mistake, saying,
"Ye Gods, you again, I meant to cut in on Dotty," or
Dede, or whoever came to his mind. I figure he knew
what he was doing. He usually does.

July 6

Heavens, what horrible trouble I am in. Bellhop Jack
wrote me a love letter and Mother went and opened it
and read it. Imagine the nerve. Anyway she called me
to her, shaking the letter at me in a most malevolent
manner. "What is the meaning of this?" she cried. I
was completely bewildered, knowing as yet nothing
of the letter and Bellhop Jack being furthest from my
thoughts. "Read this," said she in tones of wrath. I
read the letter and my hair felt like it was standing
straight up in horror. It was a terrible letter, saying
I was the itsiest girl he knew and he had great plans
for us if I would meet him in the back of the Club
at the next dance. He stated he would kiss me til I
was black and blue, and other icky things. Naturally
Mother was incensed. I tried to explain all. I said all
I did was dance with him once. It wasn't my fault he

had to go write such a gooey letter. Mother feels it was my fault, that I have no judgment and am too young to be let out of her sight for even five minutes. This will be a catastrophe for both of us. We do not get along under the most favorable of circumstances.

Then she said, "You will take this letter to him and tell him you never want to hear from him again." I shouted, "I won't do it! How can you humiliate me when it wasn't my fault?" Mother said, "You will do it, or be grounded the rest of the summer." I was really mad by then. At Mother, but mainly at Bellhop Jack for getting me in all this trouble just because I tried to be kind. "All right," I said coldly, "see if I care, but as long as I live, I will never speak to you again." Mother called for the car and actually came with me while I went through this horrendous ordeal. By this time I hated Bellhop Jack so much that I didn't even mind tearing up the letter and throwing it in his face. I felt virtuous all day long, but when I went to bed, I cried. I had been made to do something that I didn't approve of and that I felt demeaned me. Mother had no right to make me do that. I should have just ignored the whole thing.

July 7

Another letter from Bellhop Jack. He called me just another snotty kid. He said he had just been leading me on to see how dumb I was. Anyway I don't care anymore. I'm glad if I hurt his feelings. Daddy says I needn't worry as he is no longer working at the Club. Thank Goodness.

July 26

My treasure hunt. Mother let me invite four girls and five boys. Each girl chose a boy to be a team with. I chose Him, of course. There were clues hidden all over the yard, eight clues in all. The prize was two dollars apiece for the team that won. I and he would have won (as I know my way around our property better than anyone else) but a clue had blown away. Debby and Ted found it. I was glad except it was hard on him, but as Daddy pointed out later it would look queer to win at your own party. Then we had supper. Then we played the Victrola on the porch, except those dumb boys wouldn't dance but only rough-house. They are so ignorant at this age. Girls are far smarter and older and even mostly taller. I am not taller than him, thank goodness, but I am taller than

Mackey and Johnny. None of them talks like boys yet, mostly like girls. Later I heard Daddy ask Mother how the children's party went. Really and honestly I get so mad I could spit.

July 30

Tayloe and I had a harrowing experience today. Mother won't let me take my boat out if she thinks it is too windy. Fortunately what she knows about the wind is negligible. If it happens to be from the southeast it is an offshore wind, and the bay by our house remains calm. This is how it was today. I took Mother to the window that looks out over the bay. "See," I said. "There is hardly a ripple."

"All right, dear," she said kindly. "Have a good time." Little did she know she might never see me again. I didn't know that either.

Tayloe and I pushed the boat over to the other side of the point and got in. Whoosh! The wind jerked the boat in the direction of Wildwood and away we went. It was wonderful at first and we had no trouble at all going with the wind. However, when we tried to turn around to start back, it was an impossibility. The wind and waves were far too strong for our small boat. At last I decided to jump in the lake and turn the boat in the right direction by pulling on the bow while Tayloe was to use the oar in the helm. Alas, as I grabbed for the pointer, a huge wave went over my head and the rope was jerked from my hand and away went the boat with Tayloe shrieking in terror and me left in the middle of the lake in a very high sea.

I was not frightened as I am a good swimmer, and Tayloe and I have spent the summer tipping the boat over on purpose so that He will come and rescue us. Daddy says he hasn't seen my hair dry all summer and that I'm more like a muskrat than a girl (an unkind comparison but meant to be humorous). Anyway Mother had never let us go out in such a wind before. I shouted for Tayloe to sail to shore, as if she had any choice. She had to go where the boat went and it was headed for Wildwood. I started swimming after her. It was not too bad as I was swimming with the wind. As I swam I watched Tayloe and the boat being hurtled ashore and many people on shore racing toward her. Tayloe stood up, apparently in one piece, and started gesticulating wildly and pointing at me.

Quickly an Evinrude was launched in my direction. It was not a large boat and had a hard time bucking the waves, but eventually it heaved alongside me and I was pulled aboard by the seediest character I have yet to see. He was muttering out of his unshaven face about crazy god-damn kids and for the first time I felt uneasy. He had one shoulder strip hanging down and he was sick. However, he got me to shore, where Tayloe was waiting, her face a strange shade of green.

We conferred on how we should get home. Tayloe would not call her mother, being afraid, and also her mother does not have a car. If I called my mother it would be the end of my boat and that was unthinkable, so the only thing to do was call Daddy at the office. I asked the seedy man if I could use his telephone and that my father would pay him for the charge when he came for me. I guess the man was anxious to be rid of us so he took me to the phone. I got Daddy right away and told him to come at once and pick us up. Daddy was not in a good mood. He told me he had to go to a meeting and I should call Mother. I cried and told him I had almost drowned and please don't make me tell Mother. Reluctantly, after much begging, he agreed to come. It took him a half hour to get where we were and by that time he had calmed down. Also I looked as pathetic as possible, shaking with cold in my wet clothes. Daddy agreed to see my boat was picked up tomorrow and asked me what I would tell my mother. I didn't know but said I would think of something.

Luck was with me. Mother was out.

August 12

It was raining today so Dotty and I played paper dolls on our sleeping porch. This sounds like a childish game but isn't. Mother thinks it is. She smiled benignly at us when she looked out to see we were not up to something. If she only knew! My Cassandra paper doll is pregnant tho not married. Dotty got mad when I got her in this predicament because she is my best doll and as Dotty says we don't know how to get her out of this trouble and if we can't think of something I'll just have to tear her up. I suggested pretending that it had never happened, but Dotty said that isn't fair. Secretly she is jealous because my Cassandra is much prettier than her Isolde. We played for about an hour but could find no solution so we walked to the village in the rain and got a soda and read movie magazines. Tayloe has a boy paper doll called Antonio—maybe she'll let him marry Cassandra. Dotty won't let Tristan marry her as he is still in college. Such worries.

Tonight Mother and Daddy went out for dinner
and Tom took me to a movie. *Children of Divorce*—
Clara Bow. She has *it*. Anyway we took Lib's car that
she got for graduation and Tom let me drive it to the
end of the Island. He has been teaching me off and
on all summer. Naturally I will be killed if found out.
So will he.

August 15

What a catastrophe! Mother went to town this morning and I naturally assumed she would not be back
for lunch. Lib's car was just sitting out in front of
the house so I decided to drive it around the Island.
I know how perfectly well, and nothing could go
wrong if I didn't go off the Island or so I thought. I
was driving along happily and was up by the tennis
courts when I spied Mother coming home. There was
no way to avoid her. Her mouth dropped open as she
saw me and she shouted for me to stop at once. I was
nervous so stepped on the gas instead of the brake and
ran into her car. Mother was speechless with rage and
vehemently shook her finger at me. When she could
at last talk, she ordered me out of Lib's car and into
hers. We left Lib's car standing by the side of the road,
with Harold ordered to pick it up after delivering us at

home. She harangued at me so fiercely I put my fingers in my ears. She pulled them away and demanded to know what I had to say for myself. This was a stupid question. I was caught. There was nothing to say. Even if there had been, she wouldn't have listened.

The outcome of all this is that I am grounded for a week. And my father will be informed. She even stated I belonged in a reform school and she personally wouldn't be surprised if that's where I end up. Sometimes I wish I were dead.

August 19

This is my fourth day of being grounded. I was really losing my mind out of boredom, but today He landed his boat at our dock and demanded to know why I hadn't been out in mine for so long. I explained I was being punished and when I told him why he looked really impressed. He agrees, however, that it isn't fair and suggested that I call up Dotty and he would go get Ted and we could all play authors. Nothing was ever said about my not being allowed to have company so I agreed. Mother was out so I couldn't ask her if it was all right.

They came and we had a nice time playing the Victrola and playing cards and drinking pop. Mother came home and didn't get mad at all. To my astonishment it was Daddy who got mad. He came home just as they were all leaving.

"What's this?" he roared. "Clover, I thought this girl was being punished!"

"Yes, she is," cried Mother, "but the poor child has been alone for four days and I thought a little entertainment might do her good. She drives me crazy moping around the house and playing those mournful songs on the Victrola."

"You're a great one," snorted Daddy. "How do you expect her to learn if you don't stick to your guns?"

"Perhaps we were a little overly severe," murmured Mother. "A week is a long time at her age."

"That's right," hissed Daddy. "Back down but don't come crying to me next time she's in trouble."

"Mother," I cried, "I have learned my lesson. I shall never be a trouble to you again." She kissed me and told me that was all she wanted to hear. It is tacitly understood I am off bounds. My heart is so light and full, I'm the happiest, luckiest girl in the world. And I love, love, love my mother. I must say I am surprised at Daddy though.

August 30

I have accomplished quite a bit this summer. I can play "Dew, Dew, Dewy Day" and "Beloved" on the piano by heart and make them sound very jazzy. I also know all the words to "Abdul Abull Bull Amir" and "Frankie and Johnny." These are very long pieces and it took me weeks to learn all the verses. I bragged a little to Daddy about it, but all he said was, "Of what use is all this to you?" Honestly! I should think he would know what a great satisfaction it gives me. None of my friends know all this.

Saturday, September 10

I get so mad! Here it is September already and school starts next Tuesday of all things awful, and we have to move to town next Monday. *He* has already moved in.

Tuesday, September 13

School started. Eighth grade no less. There are two new girls in our class, Dorothy Simpson and Helen Archer. Helen has moved into the house next door to us. She has a sister in the seventh grade named Sissy. They are cute girls and it will be fun having them next door.

Thursday, September 15

It is droll to watch the little seventh graders trying to
adjust to high school life. Could I have been as naive
only one year ago? No, I have always been old for my
age. I feel sure I didn't have any trouble adjusting. We
have Algebra this year (I hate it) and also Science,
which is fun.

I thought it would be nice having Helen and Sissy
live next door. It isn't, though. They both pretended
they were sick and stayed home from school. I had to
carry both their books to them, plus my own. I told
them what I thought of them, lazy things. They're as
bad as Olivia. Believe me, I'm not going to carry their
books again. My arms still ache. Of all the nerve!

A fiendish person by the name of Miss Diether
teaches us Latin. She is beneath contempt and I am
paralyzed with fright of her. Oh, dear. And I thought
everything was going so well. How can I possibly
learn Latin from that cross old son-of-a-seacook.

October 1

I hate Miss Diether. I try so hard with Latin. I spend
more time on it than any other subject and I know it,
too, but whenever she calls on me in class my mind
goes blank with fear. She is very sarcastic and unat-

tractive. She says things like "If you have a mind, why don't you use it?" And I just sit there hot as fire with rage and humiliation. I have been asked to the Academy plays by Bud. If I get a card I can't go. How can I avoid it with her giving me 0 every day? I could tell Daddy how mean she is, but I hate to tattle even on her, being of a noble nature. It seems that she picks on one girl in every class she has. Woe is me that I should be the chosen one. Damn.

Monday, October 3

I didn't sleep all night, trying to think of what to do about Latin. I have to go to the Academy plays and I intend to, somehow. This morning I made up my mind. I decided to take my life in my hands and entreat Miss Diether not to give me a card. I waited til lunch hour and went to her room, where she was correcting papers. "Please, Miss Diether," I managed to utter, "please don't give me a card this week as I want to go to the Academy more than anything and won't be allowed to if I get a card." She looked at me fiercely and said she had never had such a request before. Then she asked me why I thought I deserved a card this week. I told her I had gotten 0 three different days on my oral work.

"That is true," she conceded. "However, your written work, while not exactly brilliant, is passing, and that is why I did not intend to give you a card. Remember this, though: had I felt you deserved one, no amount of begging would have changed my mind. Don't try this again." I am not so bitter about her since this display of fair play, and I'll get to go to the plays. Hot Dog!

Tuesday, October 4

My brother Tom has many girl friends, but there is one that he has liked best for almost six months. Her name is Ellie and she is little with black hair and brown eyes. She is very pretty but has a pastel personality. I like her a little, not much though. There is another girl named Dolly. Tom likes her, too, but not so much as Ellie. Anyway he writes letters to both of them, and I deliver the letters to them at school. I do not approve of this. I feel it is dishonorable of him when they each think they are his only girl. I decided I would have to put a stop to his "shenanigans" (a word of Daddy's) so on purpose I gave each girl the wrong letter. Ellie was so shocked she cried and had to stay in the restroom all morning. Dolly was only mad.

Friday, October 7

Olivia's birthday! She is nine now. Polly (our cousin) came for supper and they were taken to a movie, a great treat as Olivia seldom is allowed out at night. She has been putting on airs all day. I guess she thinks being nine is really something. It isn't, though. I wonder if I thought being nine was so marvelous. Isn't it killing?

I went to dancing school. It is fun, but I wish the boys I know could drive cars. It is humiliating to always have to be driven by Harold or one of the mothers. What I need to do is go with boys who are older. But then Mother wouldn't let me anyway, so what's the use.

October 17

Tom and I were thinking how nice it would be if we could get an apartment and live there, away from the family.

"I can wear a red sequin dress and smoke and have French heels," I said, "and we can drink cocktails every night."

"Is that all independence means to you?" queried my brother. "Remember you are only thirteen years old and I will have to be responsible for you."

"I won't be thirteen forever," I pointed out, "and anyway I don't want you bossing me around. What change would that be?" We got in quite a fight.

"Where would we get the money?" I asked practically. Then I offered generously, "I suppose I could be a lady of the night. That would bring in some money." Tom grew white, livid with rage. Even I know when I have gone too far, so I flounced out of the room remarking that under no circumstances would I ever be under his jurisdiction or anyone else's. I guess that is the end of that good idea. Neither of us has mentioned it since. He's getting to think he's so big and important. Bossing me around, really!

Friday, October 21

Tonight a friend of Tom's came for supper. His name is Jule Hannaford. I have liked him ever since I found out about a funny trick he and Tom did a couple of years ago. Mr. and Mrs. Hannaford had a dinner party at the lake. It was a hot summer evening so the table was set on the porch with a long tablecloth. It was a simple thing for Tom and Jule to run a hose under the table with a sprinkler attached. When all the guests were seated, they (Jule and Tom) turned on the faucet from outside the house.

Daddy told us no one said a word at first and all the ladies looked embarrassed as they wondered what on earth was going on. Then Mr. Hannaford shouted, "What the hell is this?" and lifted the tablecloth and found the sprinkler. Tom and Jule were long since gone, of course. Mother did not think this a funny joke. I do, though.

October 25

Helen and Sissy and I often walk home from school together. I like to stop at the drugstore and have a soda. Helen and Sissy never have any money, though, and I hate to eat mine in front of them when they can't have any. So I buy them each one, too. This is very expensive for me, coming to 45 cents a day. As I get only $5.00 a month I naturally become bankrupt. I felt it was unfair for me to have to forgo the one pleasure in my day because of them so I started charging our sodas to Daddy. I am not allowed to do this. It is now getting toward the first of the month and I am getting worried. I will probably get killed.

October 26

I worried all night about the charging and never went to sleep at all. It seemed a cruel shame for me to have to worry so about this altruistic thing I was doing for others with Daddy's money. I had one hope. Possibly if Daddy went out of town at the time the bills came in, it might pass unnoticed and I vowed to myself I would never do such a thing again, even if I had to go sodaless, if only I got away with this one time.

I could stand the suspense no longer so I went to Daddy and asked him when he was leaving town. He eyed me suspiciously and said he had no such plans. When I was crestfallen he jumped on me suddenly with the question "What have you been up to?" I figured I would be found out anyway so I merely stated, "I have been charging." Daddy demanded to know all and was most sympathetic. He said he would call the girls' father and I begged him not to, knowing they will never speak to me again. He patted my hand and stated that I was not to worry. Then he called Mr. Archer and told him he didn't think it right that his (Daddy's) poor kid had gone bankrupt because he (Mr. Archer) was too stingy to give his kids an allowance. They chortled and laughed over it and the outcome is that Helen and Sissy are to get $5.00 a month from now on and Mr. Archer said he would see that they paid for me for a change. This has worked out to the good for everybody. Nice Daddy and Nice Mr. Archer.

November 15

I haven't written much lately as I have to work so hard on my schoolwork it takes all my time. I have a horror of getting a card and then I can't go out on the weekend if I do. We have fun weekends. Every other one is dancing school, of course. Saturdays we go to the movies in a gang and then back to the Archers or our house for refreshments and dancing to the Victrola. Sundays everyone goes skating at the University Club. It is nice. I never have to worry that I won't see Him. I'm sure He likes me but He still won't admit it. He dances with me the most and teases me the most and exasperates me endlessly. I wonder if I would like him as much if I were sure of him. It wouldn't be as exciting.

November 28

Helen and I walked to school together every day. Sometimes Sissy walks with us and sometimes a girl named Ruth who goes to a different school comes with us. Today Helen and Ruth were talking about running away. They asked me to come with them. I didn't like to say no, but I really don't want to. It is too cold. I tried to tell them that and I also demanded to know where we would go and what we would do when we got there. They think they can get a job and earn a lot of money. I admit I don't adore school but it's better than working all day just to be able to eat. I persuaded them to wait until the first as I get my allowance then. I hope to heaven they forget about it by then. I don't intend to go but hate to be thought a sissy.

December 1

I had a cold today. At least I'm pretending to. Helen and Ruth are still determined to run away. They came over after school today and I gave them my allowance. I told them I was too sick to go and please to wait a while longer. (I still hoped they would forget about the whole idea.) They said they could not wait any longer. They plan to leave tomorrow. I can't tell on them and yet I feel I should stop them some way. If anything happens to them it will be on my conscience all my life. What to do?

Mother just came in and claims I look feverish. Little does she know that's the least of my troubles.

December 2

All is well. Helen and Ruth went, but only had money enough to get to Hastings. There they tried to get jobs as waitresses in a café. In the meantime Mr. Archer had them traced and they are now safely back home, thank goodness. They were gone only a little over six hours. It is interesting to know a person can be found so quickly.

December 12

Helen and Sissy came for supper tonight. Tom stayed home as he often does when he knows they are coming. He has a great fondness for Sissy. I can't understand it. She is younger than I am. She is very cute but even so it seems queer. He suggests before they come that we girls play Truth and Consequences and that I send them into the library and make them kiss him. This isn't much fun for me. I do it, though. I can't see why he likes to kiss Sissy so much. She wears braces still, and I can't think it is a very comfortable thing to do. I told Tom I was going to tell Ellie. He said if I did it would be the last thing I ever did. He has a fierce temper so I guess I won't after all.

Sunday, December 25

What a Christmas! I got new skates (my others are too small and Mother has known it since Fall). Also a new diary for next year. Lib gave me a pair of silk stockings (*not* serviceable, thank goodness).

We went to the McDonells' (our cousins) for lunch. I had to sit with the young kids. I was so disappointed. It wasn't much fun but you have to put up with lots of indignities when you are thirteen. Next year will be different though, because Auntie Onolee said as we were leaving, having noted my crestfallen appearance, "Next year, dear, you will sit at the big table with us!" It's about time somebody realized I am no mere child.

My favorite actresses are:
1. Clara Bow
2. Janet Gaynor
3. Bebe Daniels

My favorite actors are:
1. Buddy Rogers
2. Charley Farrell
3. Lon Chaney

My favorite music is:
1. "Button Up Your Overcoat"
2. "I'm on the Crest of a Wave"
3. "Red Lips"

Summary of 1927

It is now New Year's Eve of 1927. I have kept this diary for one whole year.

In looking back over this past year I feel I have become a great deal more mature. When I started this diary I was but a child in many ways, though old for my age. There are many things I did earlier in the year that seem silly to me now—like stealing the silver at school (I should have known that wouldn't work), and ringing the fire bell brought nothing but a miserable hour for me. I am glad I am doing better at school. I haven't had a card all Fall, and I actually enjoy going to class when I can answer the questions I'm supposed to know. I still like HIM but it doesn't seem so important anymore to find out if he likes me. I figure he must or he would be a moron wasting so much time trying to exasperate me. Besides, I can make him mad by ignoring him and by making scathing remarks.

I get along much better with Mother. I realize now that she is growing old (she is nearly forty-four years old). It is hard for her to see that things have changed since the olden days when she was my age. She has even conceded that perhaps for my fourteenth birthday (not too long to wait) I might expect shoes with a

Cuban heel: "not for every day, of course, dear," she said, "only for very special occasions." Still that is something.

I have found a way of putting on lipstick and then rubbing it off that leaves a little and she doesn't notice it.

And then there's Daddy. I rely on him the most. Sometimes I know it isn't convenient for him to come when I need him. He always does, though (like the time with the sailboat). He's nearly always fair except that time with the joke. I still don't get it.

My sister Olivia has grown much less obnoxious. Many times I like being with her when I have nothing else to do. She has a good sense of humor and we make up a lot of jokes about people that only we understand. We laugh a lot. I guess she is growing up.

Grandpa gets along well. He is nearly seventy-seven. Tay is still the boss of Olivia but of course she has no jurisdiction over me. Tom is going away to Hun School next year. I will miss him. Though he is nearly four years older than I am, he relies on my help and guidance in his numerous love affairs. If it weren't for me I doubt he would have a girl speaking to him. Lib is nearly nineteen now. Good heavens, that's old. Maybe she'll get married this year and I can be bridesmaid and also have her room.

But of all things that happened this year the most important was that someone thought me charming. I can't help but think so, too.

A person who is charming surely shouldn't have to worry about Him any more.

Now I must get ready to go out for New Year's Eve. We're all going over to the Archers' and we plan to call our parents every fifteen minutes all evening. They won't have time to have any fun at all.

Happy New Year, dear diary. I can't wait for 1928, can you?

Love,

"CoCo"

Coco's mother often had photographers come to the Irvine house and lake home to record her lovely, lively children. Here Coco, about five years old, wears a fur muff, fur hat, and wool winter coat with a fur collar.

The Irvine children in front of the family home circa 1915, before Olivia was born: Clotilde (Coco) Emily Irvine, Elizabeth (Libby) Irvine, and Thomas (Tom) Edward Irvine. The home on St. Paul's Summit Avenue had twenty rooms, not counting several sleeping porches for hot summer nights. *Courtesy of the Minnesota Historical Society.*

In 1917, Clotilde Irvine poses with her three eldest children, Libby, Tom, and Coco. *Courtesy of the Minnesota Historical Society.*

At Cloverdale Farm near Stillwater, Minnesota, Coco rides a fine-looking horse. She is thirteen in this photograph—the age when she was keeping her diary.

Coco *(right)* with her sister Olivia on a wicker
sofa at their home at 1006 Summit Avenue in
St. Paul. The two sisters gave their family's
mansion to the state in 1965, and it is now the
Governor's Residence. Coco, almost five years
older than Olivia, is about ten years old in this
picture, which was taken by a professional
photographer.

Clotilde Irvine, Coco's mother, in a lacy chemise
dress circa 1925, close to the time when Coco
kept her diary. Like most young teens, Coco
had mixed feelings about her parents. She
wrote in her diary: "I don't like my mother very
much but I do want her to like me." And later:
"My heart is so light and full, I'm the happiest,
luckiest girl in the world. And I love, love, love
my mother." Photograph by Moffett, Chicago.
Courtesy of the Minnesota Historical Society.

Coco's father, Horace H. Irvine, circa 1934. He was an executive with the Weyerhaeuser lumber enterprises. His mansion, built in 1910 for $50,000, features an elegant staircase and a stunning variety of wood paneling, including African mahogany in the living room. Photograph by Benjamin C. Golling. *Courtesy of the Minnesota Historical Society.*

At age thirteen, Coco recorded in her diary that she is pleased "someone special" thought her charming. The lace collar was popular at the time.

Coco, in her white dress for graduation from Summit High School, a private school in St. Paul. She has a pearl necklace and a dreamy pose—perhaps thinking of boys, still one of her favorite topics. Already weeks before her thirteenth birthday, she wrote on the first page of her 1927 diary, "Everything is getting quite different in my life because of boys! I absolutely like one now."

Beautiful even after sadness descended on her life: Coco at age twenty-seven in 1941.

Coco's wedding day in 1936 at St. John the Evangelist Episcopal Church in St. Paul. Her groom, she notes, has "a most romantic name." Attendants included her two sisters: Olivia Irvine was maid of honor and Elizabeth Fobes was matron of honor.

Afterword

PEG MEIER

So guess who Coco married! Creighton Churchill, that's who—her older sister Libby's handsome boyfriend, the one who caught her munching an apple at the front door. Yes indeed, Creighton, the love of Coco's young life. Also from a prominent, wealthy St. Paul family, he was educated at Harvard University and loved literature, history, and philosophy. On top of all that, he was a champion discus thrower. Coco found him quite the catch.

After Coco finished two years at Sarah Lawrence College in New York, where she studied writing and child development, she returned to St. Paul and renewed her friendship with Creighton. Romance followed. She was terrified that her parents would not approve of her marriage to a man almost seven years older than she. She kept her engagement ring hidden until she felt it was the right time for her fiancé to properly ask her father for her hand. Horace Irvine approved, and their wedding in the winter of 1936 was said to be the highlight of the social scene.

During the Great Depression, jobs were hard to find, even for moneyed young men, and Creighton worked for Coco's father in a contracting business until that too failed and he had to find other work. The Churchills were ecstatic with the birth of their daughter, Olivia, named for Coco's sister but always called Vicki. For the young family, life was fun and promising, as grand and exciting as Coco's had been as a teenager.

Then tragedy struck: in November 1940, a seemingly healthy Creighton died at age thirty-three of a heart attack on a hunting trip near Huron, South Dakota. Coco was only twenty-six, and their daughter, Vicki, was two. The once high-spirited Coco became depressed and anxious. Her parents begged, even ordered, her to move in with them at the Summit Avenue house, less than a mile away, but she wouldn't. She wanted to stay in her large, gracious home at 715 Goodrich Avenue, which she and Creighton had renovated and where they had been so happy.

Creighton had left her relatively little money and had no life insurance. In those times, few women of means worked outside the home, especially not upper-class widows. Coco struggled to keep the household going. She received an allowance from her parents (Vicki remembers it as $300 a month in the 1940s—somewhat less than $5,000 in today's dollars), which Coco did not find sufficient for the elegant lifestyle she was expected to keep. She wasn't especially good with money anyway. "She didn't dare tell her parents that she needed more," Vicki remembers. "She was terrified to admit it." One of Vicki's most vivid childhood memories is snuggling with her mom on a sofa in front of a sunny window, wrapped together in Coco's mink coat and reading books in the Wizard of Oz series. The reason for their cuddling together is not only sentimental: they were saving money on fuel oil, and their house was darn cold. When they were so conscious of money all the time, Coco and Vicki would feel unsettled during Sunday evening visits to Grandmother Irvine's opulent home, with four or five servants on hand and much more domestic comfort than they could afford.

Coco's sister Olivia remembered her as "always fun," but Coco's daughter saw her as much more subdued than the vivacious girl we met in the diary: "She was a very intelligent, very internal human being, quiet, frightened of a lot of things." Coco became even more insular after what Vicki describes as "a horrible, horrible experience for us." In this instance, Coco could truthfully say it happened "through no fault of my own."

It was Thursday, November 8, 1945. Vicki was in second grade at the private, upscale Summit School (now called the St. Paul Academy and Summit School). A teenage boy came to the door of Coco's home around noon, and the maid answered. He seemed to know the household and asked for Coco by name ("Mrs. Churchill"), so Coco's maid called her to the door. He then pushed his way in and showed off a black pistol. Coco recognized him as the boy she had hired the previous winter to shovel snow. She didn't remember his name.

"I have your little girl," he threatened, "and I'll kill her if I don't get your money." He took her wedding and engagement rings and two gold bracelets, and he forced the maid into the coat closet, all the time demanding $5,000. When Coco said she didn't keep that kind of money in the house, he ordered her to get into her big gray sedan parked outside and to drive him to the First National Bank for cash. That was the very building, coincidentally, where her father kept an office. Coco's little Yorkshire terrier, Peggy,

jumped into the car with them. "Don't tell anybody.
I've got some other guys in there to watch you," the
boy threatened as they approached the bank. "Don't
pull anything." He stayed with the car in a parking
lot as Coco, trembling and nearly hysterical, steeled
herself to walk into the bank. She managed to whis-
per to a teller, "I am being held up. He's in the parking
lot. Please call my father on the twenty-second floor."

Coco's maid already had called the police. Every
squad car in and near downtown St. Paul was rushed
to the bank and parking lot, the newspapers reported.
When they got to the car, officers found the door open,
the boy gone, and Coco's dog barking wildly in the
passenger seat. Coco yelled to the policemen, "He's got
my daughter, and he's going to kill her!" The *St. Paul
Dispatch* went to press that afternoon with a screaming front-page headline: ROBS, KIDNAPS SOCIALITE.

Because he had told Coco her child would be killed
"if you dare tell anyone," police assigned a guard to
watch over Vicki. Coco didn't know it, but the young
robber was acting alone and Vicki was safe at Summit
School, unaware of the turmoil. After the boy fled,
he pawned some of Coco's jewelry, hid the rest of it
under the back steps of his mother's house, and went
to the movies. He returned home at midnight, and two

detectives were waiting to arrest him. He still had the pistol on him—a toy gun. The top story in the *Pioneer Press* the next day was headlined WOMAN'S KIDNAPPER CAPTURED. It identified the boy as sixteen-year-old Ronald Lindick of 348 Superior Street. An ardent film fan who sometimes saw three or four movies a day, he told police, "I've seen robberies staged in the movies, but that isn't why I did this thing. I just had a terrible urge to get away [from home], and I thought I saw a way to do it."

He confessed and was sent to a juvenile reform school. Vicki says her mother's terror continued because the boy's mother often telephoned their house at dinnertime. In the 1940s, of course, there were no telephone-answering machines or caller-identification options: people always answered phones when they rang. Way too often at Coco's house, the boy's mother was calling to ask, "How could you do that to my son? How could you send him away?" Coco immediately hung up and crumbled emotionally every time.

Surely her husband's early death and the purported kidnapping made Coco more fearful and retiring. But Vicki also remembers her mother's courage. During World War II, Coco was a civil defense warden. At the sound of wailing sirens, she would put on her metal hat and search the neighborhood for any forbidden glimmer of light, usually leaving Vicki alone in the house. That helped Vicki toughen up, too—and contributed to her conviction that being an only child is difficult. Maybe if she had had a sibling at home with her, she could have been braver.

Vicki Churchill Ford went on to have six children and now has twenty grandchildren. She and her husband of fifty years, Si Ford, raised their children in Bronxville, New York, where Vicki serves as an elected councilwoman. The family gathers every summer on Manitou Island in White Bear Lake at the summer home of her grandparents, Horace and Clotilde Irvine. Coco rebuilt the property for year-round living in 1965, and since her death the home has been maintained for the extended family.

In 1947, Coco remarried. Her second husband, Ted Moles, was an executive with the Archer Daniels Midland Company. Vicki describes him as brusque, athletic, and an astonishingly smart and knowledgeable gentleman, but she said he had a long problem with alcohol. The family, including some of his children, lived in Coco's St. Paul house. Coco was a Brownie leader and was active in the Junior League and the women's group of her church, St. John's Episcopal. She continued to write, including a few songs, but apparently none of these stories were published. Her second husband also preceded her in death; Ted Moles died in 1970.

Of her siblings: The despondent Libby committed suicide in 1949 at age forty. Tom married Sally Ordway of the Minnesota Mining and Manufacturing Company dynasty; they were a prominent couple in the Twin Cities arts scene. Olivia married Arthur Dodge and founded the Thomas Irvine Dodge Nature Center in West St. Paul, named for their son and visited by about forty thousand people each year. The last living Irvine of her generation, Olivia died at age ninety in 2009.

Coco was transcribing her handwritten girlhood diary to a typed copy when she was ill with throat cancer in 1975. She couldn't give up her Chesterfields until near the end of her life. She died July 12, 1975, at age sixty-one, with her daughter and some grandchildren at her bedside at home in White Bear Lake. Her sister Olivia finished the diary project and presented hard-cover copies as Christmas gifts for the immediate family. Coco left clear instructions that she was to be buried in St. Paul's Oakland Cemetery, next to her beloved first husband, Creighton, under the Churchill gravestone.

Coco Irvine Moles was born in 1914, the third of four children of lumber baron Horace Irvine and his wife, Clotilde. The family lived in a twenty-room home on fashionable Summit Avenue in St. Paul, Minnesota. Coco was an intelligent girl prone to pulling pranks, and when she was thirteen she kept a diary to record her mischief. After attending college in the East, she married a man from Minnesota, and they had a daughter. Coco and her sister Olivia donated their childhood home to the State of Minnesota in 1965, and it is now the Minnesota Governor's Residence. She died in 1975.

Peg Meier was a prize-winning reporter for the Minneapolis *Star Tribune* for thirty-five years. Since her retirement, she has relished digging for fun stories in Minnesota archives. One day she found Coco's 1927 diary and started reading, stifling her laughter in the historical society library. She is the author of *Bring Warm Clothes: Letters and Photos from Minnesota's Past* and *Wishing for a Snow Day: Growing Up in Minnesota.*